Peace of
Mind®

Peace of Mind
Flex Curriculum

Grades 3

Fifteen engaging, flexible and experiential lessons that equip students with the skills to manage big emotions, learn empathy and compassion, build healthy relationships, and express emotions in American Sign Language.

Linda Ryden
Including original stories, illustrations and videos

Welcome to the Peace of Mind Community!

Peace of Mind®

Questions? Comments?
We'd love to hear from you!

Please visit teachpeaceofmind.org or
contact us at info@TeachPeaceofMind.org.

Peace of Mind Publications

Curriculum

Peace of Mind Core Curriculum for Early Childhood
Peace of Mind Core Curriculum for Grades 1 & 2
Peace of Mind Core Curriculum for Grade 3
Peace of Mind Core Curriculum for Grades 4 & 5
Peace of Mind Core Curriculum for Middle School
Peace of Mind Flex Curriculum for Kindergarten
Peace of Mind Flex Curriculum for Grades 1 & 2
Peace of Mind Flex Curriculum for Grade 3
Peace of Mind Flex Curriculum for Grade 4
Peace of Mind Flex Curriculum for Grades 5-8
Social Justice Lesson Curriculum for Grades 3-5

Storybooks

Henry is Kind
Rosie's Brain / El Cerebro de Rosita
Marleigh is Mindful / Marleigh practica la conciencia plena
Marleigh's Big Feelings
Mason and the Conflict CAT / Mason y el conflicto CAT
Quinn and the Worry Channel
Sergio Sees the Good
Tyaja Uses the Think Test

TeachPeaceofMind.org/shop/

Peace of Mind Inc. Washington DC 20015
https://TeachPeaceofMind.org
Copyright 2025 Linda Ryden and Peace of Mind Inc.

Editor: Cheryl Cole Dodwell
Cover and Interior Design: Schwa Design Group
Illustrations, Graphics and Videos: Linda Ryden
Logo: Pittny Creative
ISBN: 979-8-9998662-1-9
LCCN: 2025917680
Published 2025

Peace of Mind Flex Curriculum For Grade 3

Peace of Mind Flex At-a-Glance

Lesson	Topic	Mindfulness Practice and ASL	Materials Needed
All lessons require a way to show a short video to the class and your Kindness Pal list. Worksheets and Coloring Sheets are included with the lessons.			
1.	Introduction to Mindfulness and Kindness Pals	Four Square Breathing ASL: Happy	Four Square Breathing Coloring Sheet
2	Take Five Breathing	Four Square Breathing and Take Five Breathing ASL: Sad	Take Five Breathing Coloring Sheet and Worksheet
3	Gravity Hands	Four Square Breathing and Gravity Hands ASL: Angry	Gravity Hands Coloring Sheet
4	Squeeze and Release	Gravity Hands and Squeeze and Release ASL: Scared	Squeeze and Release Coloring Sheet
5	Flower Breathing	Squeeze and Release and Flower Breathing ASL: Silly	Flower Breath Coloring Sheet
6	Visualization	Flower Breathing and Visualization ASL: Surprised	Draw a Picture of your Peaceful Place and Visualization Coloring Sheet
7	Gratefuls	Visualization and Gratitude Practice ASL: Worried	Gratitude Coloring Sheet and Gratefuls Worksheet
8	Wave Breathing	Gratefuls and Wave Breathing ASL: Worried	Wave Breathing Drawing Worksheet
9	Make up Your own Breath	Mindfulness Helper Choice ASL: Peaceful	Create your Own Breath Worksheet
10	Sergio Sees the Good	Mindfulness Helper Choice ASL: I feel	Paper Cups, Marbles or Paper Clips, Scales Coloring Sheet
11	Tell Me Something Good	Mindfulness Helper Choice ASL: Frustrated	10 Little Good Things worksheet
12	Rosie's Brain	Mindfulness Helper Choice ASL: Excited	Brain Poster
13	Mason and the Conflict CAT	Candle breathing ASL: How are you feeling today?	Conflict CAT Poster Candle Breathing Coloring Sheet
14	Practice Conflict CAT	Mindfulness Helper Choice ASL: Hungry	Conflict CAT Poster
15	Kindness Taps	Heartfulness ASL: Loved	Heartfulness Worksheet

Introduction to the Peace of Mind Peace of Mind Flex Curriculum

Welcome to the Peace of Mind Flex Curriculum! If you are looking for a series of flexible mindfulness-based SEL lessons that can be used daily or weekly, this curriculum is for you! This Flex Curriculum is designed to be used in schools and out-of-school time programs where time or staffing constraints allow only 15-20 minutes for social and emotional learning lessons. Lessons may be broken up into modules and taught over the course of a week.

Curriculum Theory of Change

Our Theory of Change (ToC) is the same for both our Flex Curriculum and our Core Curriculum. The ToC includes our Curriculum Pillars, Learning Experiences, Core Teaching Practices, and the Outcomes we hope to see for students. Here it is:

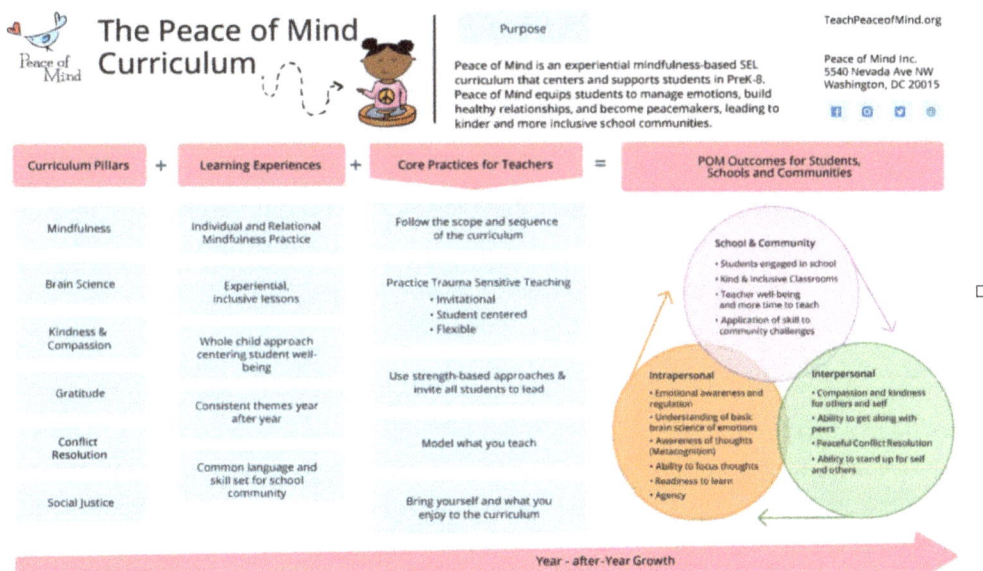

Pillars

The Flex Curriculum is built on Peace of Mind's 6 foundational pillars: Mindfulness, Brain Science, Kindness and Compassion, Gratitude, Conflict Resolution and Social Justice. Engaging and fun, this mini-series uses animated stories and mindfulness practice videos along with interactive discussions and activities to engage students in:

- Experiencing mindfulness practice for themselves;
- Learning what happens in their brains when they experience a big emotion;
- Learning how mindful practices can affect their ability to respond;
- Learning how mindfulness can help in resolving conflicts peacefully.

Every lesson ends with Kindness Pals, a pair practice that helps students get to know each other and build a caring classroom community in a relatively short time.

Learning Experiences

This Flex Curriculum, like our Core Curriculum, is designed to promote learning experiences that center student well-being and agency while supporting a kind and inclusive classroom and school community. You'll notice that students learn mindfulness not only for themselves, but for their relationships with others. The curriculum is experiential and inclusive with opportunities for student leadership and personal growth throughout. Schools that use Peace of Mind year-after-year in all grade levels will find consistent themes with age-appropriate lessons. Peace of Mind also helps school communities to develop a common language and skill set related to our own well-being, building healthy relationships, and solving conflicts peacefully.

Outcomes

When taught with fidelity, The Peace of Mind Flex Curriculum will help students to:

- Increase their self-awareness and self-regulation;
- Understand the basic science related to their emotions;
- Regularly practice kindness, compassion and gratitude;
- Be more aware of and more skillfully focus their thoughts;
- Build positive relationships with peers and adults;
- Build kind and inclusive classrooms.

Core Teaching Practices

Through our work with partner schools and academic researchers, we have identified five core teaching practices for effective, impactful implementation of Peace of Mind.

1. **Follow the Scope and Sequence of the Curriculum**

   This lesson sequence is designed to first give students a foundational set of mindfulness practices to help them manage their emotions and learn to put space between their reactions to a big feeling and their response. Gratitude practice follows and an introduction to one aspect of how our brains work: our negativity bias. Students learn more basic brain science in the lesson on Rosie's Brain. The curriculum, like every lesson, closes with kindness practice. With this foundation, students are ready for the conflict resolution lessons.

   - **Mindfulness**
     In all lessons, students learn and practice mindfulness exercises,

building their own tool kit to help them notice and manage big emotions. Students experience the effects of each practice personally and begin to discern which practices are most helpful to them.

- **Gratitude**
  We explore gratitude in several different ways including our brain's tendency to focus on the negative and how gratitude practice helps to balance this tendency by focusing on small good things we experience. Through stories, games and activities, students experience this for themselves.

- **Brain Science**
  Through the Rosie's Brain story, students gain powerful insight into what happens in our brains when we get angry and why mindfulness helps us calm down.

- **Conflict Resolution**
  Building on the foundation laid in earlier lessons, students learn to use mindfulness and a new understanding of their brains to understand when they are in a conflict and how they can use their skills to calm down, apologize and work out a peaceful solution.

- **Kindness and Compassion**
  We end the curriculum with a focus on self-compassion and compassion for others, making a Kindness Chain as a final way of connecting with and appreciating each other.

- **Social Justice**
  Former U.S. Surgeon General Vivek Murthy said that "mental health is the defining public health crisis of our time." The ultimate goal of the Peace of Mind Program is to create a kinder, more peaceful world with and for our children. We begin by helping to create classroom communities where students feel loved and seen. We help children and their grownups learn how to recognize and manage their emotions, how to feel compassion for others and themselves and how to work out conflicts peacefully. We hope that with these personal and interpersonal skills, children will grow up to find peaceful solutions to the most challenging social justice issues of our time.

2. **Practice Trauma Sensitive Teaching**

You will notice in the lesson scripts three important components of trauma-sensitive teaching:

- **Invitational** - Mindfulness practice is always invitational. While we expect everyone to sit together during the mindful moments, we invite students to choose whether or not to engage with a practice. They

can choose for themselves, but they cannot interfere with someone else's choice. We ask everyone to be respectful of others while making their own decision about whether to do a practice or not. Students are welcome to just sit quietly.

- **Student-centered** - We teach mindfulness practices for students' own well-being. We teach a variety of practices not so students can master them all, but so they can find the ones that work best for them. If a student is having a hard time with a practice, suggest that they choose another one that works better for them.

- **Flexible** - We don't require students to close their eyes or sit in a certain way to practice. If students need to make modifications to a practice (keeping their eyes open or walking quietly in the back of the room, for example) to help themselves feel comfortable this is fine as long as their choices do not interfere with others' comfort and safety.

3. **Use Strength-Based Approaches**

You will notice that the scripts offered for the lessons use strength-based language: language that focuses on students' abilities, interests and potential, not deficits. The curriculum is designed to promote student agency and leadership, especially through the role of Mindfulness Helper. The Mindfulness Helper is a student who leads the class in the mindfulness practice for the day. Here's how it works:

- The teacher consults their alphabetical roll list and chooses a student to be the Mindfulness Helper (MH) for the day.

- The teacher encourages the class to offer sign language applause for the person who is chosen that day.

- The MH can sit near the teacher.

- With the teacher's help the MH says slowly, "Let's get into our mindful bodies.... Let's close our eyes or look down. ... Let's Invite three deep breaths." Always offer the students a choice about keeping their eyes open or closed. At this point the teacher will lead the rest of the mindfulness practice as instructed in the lesson.

- The MH rings the bell/chime when the mindfulness practice is complete.

- The teacher then asks the MH to return to their seat.

- You will need to help students remember what to say at the beginning of the year. Repeating the same words each class is important to help students develop a routine to help them begin to practice on their own.

Read more about this on Page 9 of the Core Curriculum for Grades 1&2.

4. **Model What You Teach**

   We know from research and our own experience that modeling what we are teaching is one of the most effective ways of engaging our students in mindfulness practice themselves. Students Invite their cues from you. You don't have to be an expert in mindfulness, but it is important to join your students on the journey.

5. **Bring Yourself to the Curriculum**

   Once you are comfortable with the first four core teaching practices, we hope you will be able to bring yourself to the curriculum. If the script isn't quite how you would say things, please adapt so you feel comfortable. If you enjoy singing, bring that in! If you enjoy crafts, make that a part of what you do. If puppets are your thing, they're welcome!

Setting Expectations

The *Peace of Mind* curriculum plants seeds of mindfulness and compassion. These seeds grow and mature inside a student's mind and heart, positively affecting the way a person sees the world and operates within it. For some students, the outward positive effects are manifested quickly and clearly. For other students, it may take more time, and the outward signs of change may be subtle. All that we expect of students is to try to practice the skills in this curriculum as often as they can —just to try.

Some students have a much easier time sitting quietly than others. Keep your expectations reasonable. Sometimes a student who is sitting with their eyes wide open, legs jiggling, and fiddling with a pencil—but not talking—during mindfulness practice is doing their very best and is benefiting greatly from the effort. That's okay. The exercises in this curriculum are for the benefit of the children and, as long as they are not preventing other children from practicing, a little wiggling around is okay.

Try to put the guidelines in positive language such as "As long as you follow the directions you can continue to play the game." This can be much more effective than the more traditional way of saying, "If you don't follow the rules you can't play." Many children react negatively to orders like that but are perfectly happy to follow the rules when they are stated in a more neutral way.

Materials Needed

- **Lesson** Slides. Accessible through QR code here:

- **Storybooks**

  Rosie's Brain, Sergio Sees the Good, and *Mason and the Conflict CAT* either in print copies or video read-alouds (links included in lessons)

- **Worksheet and Coloring Sheet Copies**

  You will find related coloring sheets and worksheets right after each lesson. Please print what you need for your class. See "At-A-Glance" to easily find what you need for each lesson.

  > *Here's an idea!* Send coloring sheets home after each class so that parents know what their children are learning in Peace Class. Or, turn the Coloring Sheets into a book for your students to Invite home at the end of the session!

- **Chime (optional)**

American Sign Language

A new addition to the Peace of Mind Curriculum, American Sign Language is a wonderful tool to use to help all children, regardless of English proficiency, learn about, explore and communicate their emotions. These lessons offer a very basic, simple introduction to expressing emotions in American Sign Language. The ASL included in these lessons is just an introduction to a rich language that can be used to communicate with students who are deaf and hard of hearing or who have other communication challenges.

For more information about learning ASL please visit:
www.nad.org/resources/american-sign-language/
learning-american-sign-language

A Note on Kindness Pals

Kindness Pals is an engaging and powerful activity that takes place every class period. Kindness Pal practice reminds children to make kindness part of their daily lives. Doing kind things for their Kindness Pals spills over into their treatment of others and so they can develop the habit of treating people with kindness through regular practice. Kindness Pals also gives children opportunities to get to know each other and to connect with others whom they might not have gotten along with in the past or whom they think they just don't like. Here's a quick video introduction to Kindness Pals.

Here is how it works:

- For each class, assign each student one Kindness Pal. You can pair up children in advance to ensure there aren't any repeated partnerships.

- When each child hears their Kindness Pal's name, emphasize that both pals, or the whole class, must say "Okay." **This is very important.** This response lets the teacher know that they have heard their assignment and that they know who their Kindness Pal is. Please practice this routine with your class. (**Watch this** <u>video</u> of kids doing Kindness pals.)

- Please let the class know that this is not a time for them to let the teacher or the class know how they feel about having that Kindness Pal. This avoids hurt feelings and also offers multiple chances to remind the children that they have the power to be kind and the power to hurt people's feelings. It all depends on their choices. This is a powerful lesson.

- Explain to the students that they will each receive one Kindness Pal each class period (or each week if you choose). Kindness Pals will participate in an activity together during the class period.

- You may also invite the students to do small kind things for their assigned Kindness Pals before the next class. Some examples of kind behavior might be to get a Pal's snack, stack their chair, or play together at recess. The following class, allow a few minutes for children to talk about what they did for their Pal.

- Kindness Pals sharing time is a perfect time to practice mindful listening. It's important to demonstrate how we listen mindfully with our whole bodies. You might even want to let a student lead the sharing.

- Assign new pals at the end of each class (or week).

Lesson 1
Introduction to Mindfulness and Kindness Pals

Slides: 1-12

1. Welcome to Peace of Mind!

You might say: *We're going to be learning about something called mindfulness. Have you ever heard of mindfulness before? What do you think it means?* **Invite some answers.**

Mindfulness means to pay attention, and we can pay attention to many different things. Mindfulness can also be about using our breath to help us take care of ourselves. How do you breathe when you run around for a long time? How do you breathe when you are scared? How do you breathe when you are nervous?

Today we're watching a video about a girl named Marleigh who we're going to be getting to know in Peace of Mind Class. She's a really good dancer, but she gets nervous when she has to perform in front of an audience. Do you ever get nervous? Let's see what Marleigh does when she gets nervous.

2. Mindful Moment

Show Marleigh Four Square Video. Marleigh introduces mindfulness and teaches the first practice.

Try Four Square Breathing with the class. **Try** taking 3 breaths this way.

Discuss: *Does breathing this way make you feel any differently? Is it hard to hold your breath? Can you do it gently? Why do you think Four Square Breathing helped Marleigh feel less nervous about her performance? How do you feel?*

3. American Sign Language (ASL)

You might say: *We're going to be learning a new way to share our feelings with each other called American Sign Language or ASL. ASL is a visual language - a language that we see with our eyes instead of listening to with our ears.*

When we use ASL, we use our facial expressions, hand signals and body movements instead of saying words with our voices. Most of the people who use ASL are deaf, which means that they cannot hear with their ears, or hard

of hearing, which means they have trouble hearing with their ears. But lots of other people use it too. Once we learn how to share our feelings in ASL we'll start using it to share our feelings with each other.

We're going to start out by learning how to say "happy." How do you feel in your body when you are happy?

Choose a few volunteers to demonstrate what "happy" looks like.

Let's watch a video of one of the Peace of Mind students showing us how to sign "happy." **Happy Video (the video is in the slides)**

4. Introduce Kindness Pals

You might say: *Now we're going to do something fun called Kindness Pals. Every class we're going to get a new Kindness Pal. Your Kindness Pal is somebody that you will get to know a little bit better. You get to do kind things for them, and they get to do kind things for you.*

Then, next time you'll get a new Kindness Pal. There's one important rule of Kindness Pals. When I tell you who your Kindness Pal is I want you to say, 'Okay!' in a nice friendly way. Let's try that together!

Are you always going to feel really excited about who you got? Maybe not. And that's okay. But how do you think we will make our Kindness pal feel if we say, 'Aw!' or, 'Rats!' or, 'But I wanted Lily!' That's right, they'll feel really bad.

Since this is your Kindness Pal it's your job to be kind to them - just for one day. So, the first kind thing you're going to do for them is to say, "Okay!"

*Let's **watch** a quick video about Kindness Pals!*

Assign Kindness Pals
Remind the students to say, "Okay!". You can make a list ahead of time or put their names on popsicle sticks and pull them randomly out of a jar. However you want to do them is fine. Just make sure that they get a different child each time **and** that they say, "Okay!"

Kindness Pal Activity
Now we're going to do an activity with your Kindness Pal. When I say "Go!" you're going to find your Kindness Pal and then I'm going to give you 30

seconds to find out how many things you have in common - how many things are the same about you. You can ask each other about foods you like, animals, colors, books, movies, toys, whatever!

Share what they have in common.

You might ask: *Who thinks they have the most things in common?* Have everyone share one thing that they had in common with their Kindness Pal.

Now for the rest of the day see if you can find any more things you have in common and try to do some kind things for your Kindness Pal.

5. **Optional: Four Square Breathing Coloring Sheet (follows lesson)**

6. **Closing**

   Let's take a moment to think about something kind you could do for your Kindness Pal today. You can close your eyes if you want to.
   Wait.
   Ask: *Who has an idea already of what you might do?* **Invite a few answers.**
   Say: *Thanks for a great class, everyone!*
   Ring a bell or chime if you have one.

   _____

   Extension: *Peace of Mind Core Curriculum for Grade 3 Lesson 1: Mindful Listening, page 22. Try Mindful Listening, another way to connect with what's going on around us and to focus our attention.*

Four Square Breathing

Hold your breath 1, 2, 3, 4 →

Breathe in, 1, 2, 3, 4 ↑

Breathe out 1, 2, 3, 4 ↓

← Wait 1, 2, 3, 4

Peace of Mind®

Lesson 2
Take Five Breathing

Slides: 13-23

1. Introduction

You might say: *Today we are going to learn another mindfulness practice and review the one we learned last time. We're going to spend some time with our new Kindness Pal and we're also going to introduce something called the Mindfulness Helper. The Mindfulness Helper will get to help me lead the mindfulness practices that we'll learn in each lesson.*

2. Mindful Moment

Choose the Mindfulness Helper

From now on you will choose a student to be the Mindfulness Helper for each class. That student will come up front to sit or stand next to you and help you to lead a mindfulness practice. If you have a little bell or chime you can let the Mindfulness Helper ring it at the end of the mindfulness practice.

Review Four Square Breathing.
Ask if anybody remembers how to do Four Square Breathing.
Choose a Mindfulness Helper and ask them to lead it with your help.

Have the Mindfulness Helper say: *"Let's get into our mindful bodies. Let's close our eyes or look down. Let's do Four Square Breathing."*

> **NOTE:** *It's important <u>not</u> to require students to close their eyes or sit in a particular way. As long as the students are not bothering each other they are fine.*

Then practice a few rounds of Four Square Breathing. Have the Mindfulness Helper ring a bell or chime if you have one - not necessary!

Learn a new mindfulness practice with Marleigh's little brother Mason called Take Five Breathing. **Watch the video**

Try Take Five Breathing with the class.

|

Discuss

Does breathing this way make you feel any differently?

Did Take Five Breathing help Mason?

Have you ever been mad about having to clean up when you wanted to play?

How could Take Five Breathing help you?

3. American Sign Language (ASL)

You might say: *Today we're going to learn how to say "sad" in ASL. How do you feel in your body when you are sad?*

Choose a few volunteers to demonstrate what "sad" looks like.

Let's watch a video of one of the Peace of Mind students showing us how to sign "sad." **(the video is in the slides)**

ASL Practice: Have everyone try to say "sad" in ASL. Point out that the sign for "sad" involves our faces, hand gestures and body motions. Ask them if the sign for "sad" matches the way that they feel when they are sad.

4. Kindness Pals

Assign new Kindness Pals. You can make a list ahead of time, or put their names on popsicle sticks and pull them randomly out of a jar, however you want to do them is fine. Just make sure that they get a different child each time and that they say "Okay!"

You might say: *Remember, every class we're going to get a new Kindness Pal. Your Kindness Pal is somebody that you will get to know a little bit better and you get to do kind things for them. Then next time you'll get a new Kindness Pal. There's one important rule of Kindness Pals. Does anybody remember what it is? When I tell you who your Kindness Pal is I want you to say "Okay!" in a nice friendly way.*

Kindness Pal Activity

Now we're going to do an activity with your Kindness Pal. When I say "Go!" you're going to find your Kindness Pal and you're going to play the Mirror Game.

We're going to be moving mindfully and really focusing on what our Kindness Pal is doing. What do you think it means to move mindfully? **Invite a few answers.**

Moving mindfully just means to really pay attention to how your body is moving.

Here's how to play the Mirror Game.

Choose a volunteer to demonstrate the Mirror Game with you.

You are going to take turns being the leader and doing slow movements with your body. Your Kindness Pal will try to be your reflection in the mirror and do the exact same movements. After one minute I will ask you to switch and the other person will be the leader.

5. Optional drawing activities

- Take Five Breathing Coloring Sheet (follows lesson)
- Trace your hand and decorate it to help you remember how to do Take Five Breathing.(worksheet follows lesson)

6. Closing

Let's take a moment to think about something kind you could do for your Kindness pal today. You can close your eyes if you want to.
Wait.
Ask: *Who has an idea already of what you might do?* **Invite a few answers.**
Say: *Thanks for a great class, everyone!*
Ring a bell or chime if you have one.

Extension: *Peace of Mind Core Curriculum for Grade 3: Lesson 15, page Page 93. Practice Tummy Breaths, another way to notice our breathing and calm our nervous system.*

Take Five Breathing

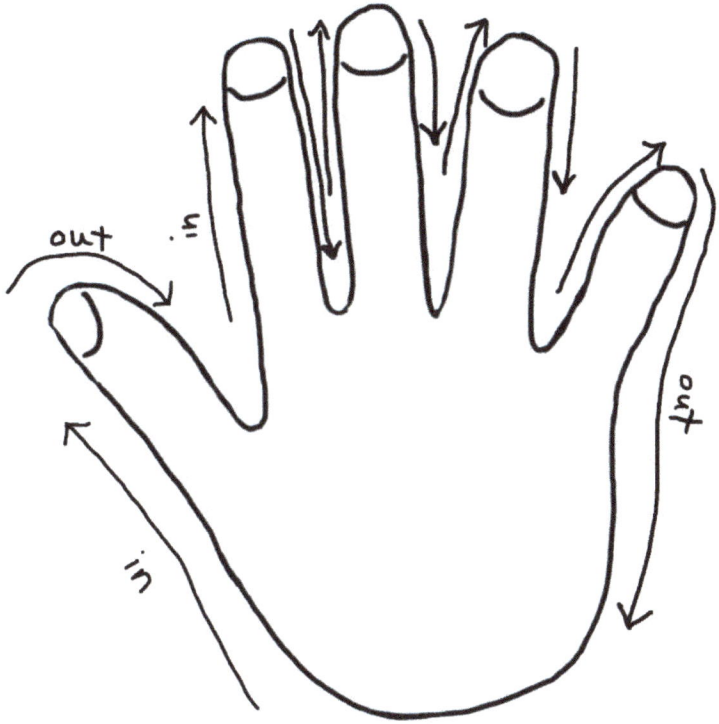

Slowly trace your hand breathing in as you
trace up and out as you trace down.

Take Five Breathing

Trace your hand and then decorate it to help you remember how to do Take Five Breathing.

Lesson 3
Gravity Hands

Slides: 25-34

1. Introduction

You might say: *Today we are going to learn another mindfulness practice and review the one we learned last time. We're also going to talk about food with our Kindness Pals.*

2. Mindful Moment

Ask if anybody remembers how to do Take Five Breathing.

Choose the Mindfulness Helper and have them lead Take Five Breathing.
Remind the MH to say, *"Let's get into our mindful bodies. Let's close our eyes or look down* (it's important not to require students to close their eyes). *Let's do Take Five Breathing."*
Practice a few rounds of Take Five Breathing.
Ring a bell or chime (or let the Mindfulness Helper ring it) if you have one - not necessary!

Learn a new mindfulness practice with Navaneet called **Gravity Hands.**
Watch the video. Try Gravity Hands with the class.

Discuss
Does breathing this way make you feel any differently? How did Gravity Hands help Navaneet? Why do you think we call it Gravity Hands?

3. American Sign Language (ASL)

You might say: *Today we're going to learn how to say "angry" in ASL. How do you feel in your body when you are angry?*

Choose a few volunteers to demonstrate what "angry" looks like.

Let's watch a video of one of the Peace of Mind students showing us how to sign "angry." **(the video is in the slides)**

ASL Practice

Have everyone try to say "angry" in ASL. Point out that the sign involves our faces, hand gestures and body motions. Ask them if the sign for "angry" matches the way that they feel when they are angry.

4. Kindness Pals

Assign New Kindness Pals: *Okay it's time to get our new Kindness Pals! There's one important rule of Kindness Pals. Does anybody remember what it is? When I tell you who your Kindness Pal is I want you to say "Okay!" in a nice friendly way.*

Kindness Pal Activity: *Okay when I say go you're going to find your Kindness Pal and you're going to talk about food! Ask each other what is one of your favorite things to eat for breakfast, lunch, dinner and dessert. You've got one minute! Go!*

Share: *Now you're going to vote with your feet. This corner is for people who like sweet foods the best. The other corner is for people who like salty foods the best. Ready? Go!*

5. Optional: Gravity Hands Coloring Sheet (follows lesson)

6. Closing

Let's take a moment to think about something kind you could do for your Kindness pal today. You can close your eyes if you want to.
Wait. Ask: *Who has an idea already of what you might do?* **Invite a few answers.**
Say: *Thanks for a great class, everyone!*
Ring a bell or chime if you have one.

Extension: *Peace of Mind Core Curriculum for Grade 3: Lesson 10, Page 66. Try the Thought Catcher Game to help students develop the ability to focus their thoughts.*

Gravity Hands

Slowly move your hands up
and down as you breathe in
and out.

Lesson 4
Squeeze and Release

Slides: 35-44

1. Introduction

You might say: *Today we are going to learn another mindfulness practice and review the one we learned last time. We're going to spend some time with our new Kindness Pal finding out what we have in common.*

2. Mindful Moment

Ask if anybody remembers how to do Gravity Hands.

Choose the Mindfulness Helper and have them lead Gravity Hands.
Remind them to say, *"Let's get into our mindful bodies. Let's close our eyes or look down* (it's important not to require students to close their eyes). *Let's do Gravity Hands."* **Practice** a few rounds of Gravity Hands.
Ring a bell or chime if you have one - not necessary!

Ask if anybody remembers how to do Four Square Breathing. Choose someone to demonstrate. Have somebody demonstrate Take Five Breathing.

Learn a new mindfulness practice with August called **Squeeze and Release.**
Watch the video. **Try** Squeeze and Release with the class.

Discuss
Does squeezing and releasing your body this way make you feel any differently? How did Squeeze and Release help August?

3. American Sign Language (ASL)

You might say: *Today we're going to learn how to say "scared" in ASL. How do you feel in your body when you feel scared?*

Choose a few volunteers to demonstrate what "scared" looks like.

Let's watch a video of one of the Peace of Mind students showing us how to sign "scared." **(the video is in the slides)**

ASL Practice

Have everyone try to say "scared" in ASL. Point out that the sign for scared involves our faces, hand gestures and body motions. Ask them if the sign for scared matches the way that they feel when they are scared.

4. Kindness Pals

Assign New Kindness Pals

Remind the students to say "Okay!" and make sure everyone is getting someone new today.

You might say: *Okay it's time to get our new Kindness Pals! There's one important rule of Kindness Pals. Does anybody remember what it is? When I tell you who your Kindness Pal is I want you to say "Okay!" in a nice friendly way.*

Kindness Pal Activity

Now we're going to do an activity with your Kindness Pal. When I say "Go!" you're going to find your Kindness Pal and then I'm going to give you 30 seconds to find out how many things you have in common - how many things are the same about you. You can ask each other about foods you like, animals, colors, books, movies, toys, whatever!

Share

Who thinks they have the most things in common? Have everyone share one thing that they had in common with their Kindness Pal. *Now for the rest of the day see if you can find any kind things to do for your Kindness Pal.*

5. Optional: Gravity Hands Coloring Sheet (follows lesson)

6. Closing

Let's take a moment to think about something kind you could do for your Kindness pal today. You can close your eyes if you want to. **Wait**.

Ask: *Who has an idea already of what you might do?* ***Invite a few answers.***

Say: *Thanks for a great class, everyone!* **Ring** a bell or chime if you have one.

Extension: *Peace of Mind Core Curriculum for Grade 3: Lesson 16 Page 98. Another way to tune into our bodies: The Walk, Stop, Wiggle, Sit game.*

Squeeze and Release

Slowly squeeze and
release parts of your body
as you breathe in and out

|

Lesson 5
Flower Breathing

Slides: 45-54

1. Introduction

You might say: *Today we are going to learn another mindfulness practice and review the one we learned last time. We're going to spend some time with our new Kindness Pal playing a game called "Switcheroo!"*

2. Mindful Moment

Ask if anybody remembers how to do Squeeze and Release.

Choose the Mindfulness Helper and have them lead Squeeze and Release.
Remind them to say, *Let's get into our mindful bodies. Let's close our eyes or look down* (it's important not to require students to close their eyes). *Let's do* Squeeze and Release.
Practice a few rounds of Squeeze and Release.
Ring a bell or chime if you have one.

Ask if anybody remembers how to do the other practices you've been learning. Ask them to demonstrate briefly.

Learn a new mindfulness practice with Josie and Cybbie called **Flower Breathing. Watch the video. Try** Flower Breathing with the class.

Discuss: *How does Flower Breathing make you feel? How did Flower Breathing help Josie?*

3. American Sign Language (ASL)

You might say: *Today we're going to learn how to say "silly" in ASL. How do you feel in your body when you feel silly?*

Choose a few volunteers to demonstrate what "silly" looks like.

Let's watch a video of one of the Peace of Mind students showing us how to sign "silly." **(the video is in the slides)**

ASL Practice

Have everyone try to say "silly" in ASL. Point out that the sign involves our faces, hand gestures and body motions. Ask them if the sign matches the way that they feel when they feel silly.

4. Kindness Pals

Assign New Kindness Pals: Remind the students to say "Okay!" and make sure everyone is getting someone new today.

You might say: *It's time to get our new Kindness Pals! There's one important rule of Kindness Pals. Does anybody remember what it is? When I tell you who your Kindness Pal is, I want you to say "Okay!" in a nice friendly way.*

Kindness Pal Activity: *When I say go, you're going to find your Kindness Pal and play Switcheroo!*

Choose a volunteer to model how to play the game.

You might say: *You and your partner will observe each other for one minute, then turn your backs to each other and switch one thing. Turn around and take turns guessing what has changed about their partner. Ready? Go!*

Ideas: Change your hair a little bit, roll down or up your sleeve, untie your shoe, pull up your sock. If they seem ready, you can up the challenge by changing **two** things.

5. Optional: Flower Breathing Coloring Sheet (follows lesson)

6. Closing

Let's take a moment to think about something kind you could do for your Kindness pal today. You can close your eyes if you want to.
Wait.
Ask: *Who has an idea already of what you might do?* ***Invite a few answers.***
Say: *Thanks for a great class, everyone!*
Ring a bell or chime if you have one.

———————————

Extension: *Peace of Mind Core Curriculum for Grade 3, Lesson 2, Mindful Listening and Mindful Seeing*

Flower Breaths

Imagine you have a flower.
Smell the flower for four counts.
Blow the petals for four counts.

Lesson 6
Visualization

Slides: 55-64

1. Introduction

You might say: *Today we are going to learn a different kind of mindfulness practice and review the one we learned last time. Instead of focusing on Mindful Breathing we're going to be using our imaginations to travel to a Peaceful Place. Then we'll share about our Peaceful Place with our Kindness Pal and if we have time we'll draw a picture of it.*

2. Mindful Moment

Ask if anybody remembers how to do Flower Breathing.

Choose the Mindfulness Helper and have them lead Flower Breathing.
Remind them to say, *"Let's get into our mindful bodies. Let's close our eyes or look down (it's important not to require students to close their eyes). Let's do Flower Breathing."* **Practice** a few rounds of Flower Breathing.
Ring a bell or chime if you have one.

Ask if anybody remembers how to do the other practices you've been learning. Ask them to demonstrate briefly.

Learn a new mindfulness practice with Malachi called Visualization. **Watch the video. Try** Visualization with the class.

Discuss: *Do you think Visualization would help you fall asleep? Could it be helpful at other times?*

3. Kindness Pals – Part 1

Assign New Kindness Pals. You might say: *Okay it's time to get our new Kindness Pals! There's one important rule of Kindness Pals. Does anybody remember what it is? When I tell you who your Kindness Pal is I want you to say "Okay!" in a nice friendly way.*

4. American Sign Language (ASL)

You might say: *Today we're going to learn how to say "surprised" in ASL. How do you feel in your body when you feel surprised?*

Choose a few volunteers to demonstrate what "surprised" looks like.

Let's watch a video of one of the Peace of Mind students showing us how to sign "surprised" **(the video is in the slides)**

ASL Practice

Have everyone try to say "surprised" in ASL. Point out that the sign involves our faces, hand gestures and body motions. Ask them if the sign matches the way that they feel when they are surprised.

5. Kindness Pals – Part 2

Kindness Pal Activity: *Okay when I say go you're going to find your Kindness Pal and take turns telling each other about what you visualized. What is in your peaceful place?*

Share: Give the class a chance to share about their Peaceful Place.

6. Optional: Visualization Coloring Sheet and Peaceful Place Drawing Sheet.

7. Closing

Let's take a moment to think about something kind you could do for your Kindness pal today. You can close your eyes if you want to.
Wait. Ask: *Who has an idea already of what you might do?* ***Invite a few answers.***
Say: *Thanks for a great class, everyone!*
Ring a bell or chime if you have one.

_____

Extension: *Peace of Mind Core Curriculum for Grade 3, Lesson 5, another guided visualization practice.*

Visualization

Imagine you are in a peaceful place.
Imagine what you would see, hear,
taste, smell and feel in that place.

Draw a picture of your
Peaceful Place

What did you see, hear, smell, taste, touch, and feel?

Lesson 7
Gratefuls

Slides: 65-75

1. Introduction

You might say: *Today we are going to learn another kind of mindfulness practice and review the one we learned last time. Today's practice is about Gratitude or the feeling of being thankful. We're going to spend some time with our new Kindness Pal sharing about things we are grateful or thankful for.*

2. Mindful Moment

Ask if anybody remembers how to do Visualization.

Choose the Mindfulness Helper and have them lead a brief Visualization practice. **Remind** them to say, *"Let's get into our mindful bodies. Let's close our eyes or look down. (It's important not to require students to close their eyes). Let's do Visualization.*
Ring a bell or chime if you have one.

Ask if anybody remembers how to do one or two of the other practices we've been learning. Ask them to demonstrate briefly.

Learn a new mindfulness practice with Peyton called Gratefuls. **Watch the video.** The students can practice with Peyton during the video. You may want to pause the video to give them more time to think.

Discuss: *What was Peyton grateful for? What did you think of that you are grateful for?*

3. American Sign Language (ASL)

You might say: *Today we're going to learn how to say "peaceful" in ASL. How do you feel in your body when you feel peaceful?*

Choose a few volunteers to demonstrate what "peaceful" looks like.

Let's watch a video of one of the Peace of Mind students showing us how to sign "peaceful." **(the video is in the slides)**

ASL Practice

Have everyone try to say "peaceful" in ASL. Point out that the sign involves our faces, hand gestures and body motions. Ask them if the sign matches the way that they feel when they feel peaceful.

4. Kindness Pals

Assign New Kindness Pals. You might say: *Okay it's time to get our new Kindness Pals! There's one important rule of Kindness Pals. Does anybody remember what it is? When I tell you who your Kindness Pal is I want you to say "Okay!" in a nice friendly way.*

Kindness Pal Activity: *When I say go, you're going to find your Kindness Pal and share three things you are grateful for. Then you can do the Gratefuls worksheet together.*

5. Optional: Gratitude Coloring Sheet. If you have time you could make Gratefuls Boxes out of shoeboxes or brown paper bags.

6. Closing

Let's take a moment to think about something kind you could do for your Kindness pal today. You can close your eyes if you want to.
Wait
Ask *Who has an idea of what you might do?* **Invite a few answers.**
Thanks for a great class, everyone!
Ring a bell or chime if you have one.

———————————————

Extension: *The Peace of Mind Core Curriculum for Grade 3: Lesson 6, page 48. This lesson includes the Cup of Gratitude Practice, another way of focusing on gratitude.*

What would you put in
your Gratefuls Box?

Draw or write your ideas below

Gratitude

Think of little things you are grateful
for. Write them down and save them
to read later.

Lesson 8
Wave Breathing

Slides: 76-85

1. Introduction

You might say: *Today we are going to learn another mindfulness breathing practice called Wave Breaths and review the one we learned last time. Then you and your Kindness Pal will get to make up your own version of Wave Breaths.*

2. Mindful Moment

Ask if anybody remembers how to do Gratefuls.

Choose the Mindfulness helper and have them lead a brief Gratitude practice.

Remind them to say, *"Let's get into our mindful bodies. Let's close our eyes or look down* (it's important not to require kids to close their eyes). *Let's think of three things we are grateful for."*

Ring a bell or chime if you have one.

Ask if anybody remembers how to do the other practices you've been learning. Ask them to demonstrate briefly.

Learn a new mindfulness practice with Silvia called Wave Breaths. **Watch the video**

Discuss. You might say: *What did you notice is different about Silvia from the other kids we've learned from? (she's a real kid, not a cartoon!) Silvia is a real kid who loves mindfulness. She loves to make up her own ways of taking her deep breaths.*

Ask: *Can you think of your own way to do Wave Breaths?"*

Invite a few kids to share their ideas and encourage the other kids to try them out. Everyone will have a chance to share with their Kindness Pal.

3. American Sign Language (ASL)

You might say: *Today we're going to learn how to say "worried" in ASL. How do you feel in your body when you feel worried?*

Choose a few volunteers to demonstrate what "worried" looks like.

Let's watch a video of one of the Peace of Mind students showing us how to sign "worried." **(the video is in the slides)**

ASL Practice

Have everyone try to say "worried" in ASL. Point out that the sign involves our faces, hand gestures and body motions. Ask them if the sign matches the way that they feel when they feel worried.

4. Kindness Pals

Assign New Kindness Pals. You might say: *It's time to get our new Kindness Pals! There's one important rule of Kindness Pals. Does anybody remember what it is? When I tell you who your Kindness Pal is, I want you to say "Okay!" in a nice friendly way.*

Kindness Pal Activity

When I say go, you're going to find your Kindness Pal and you and your Kindness Pal are going to share your own way of doing Wave breaths and teach them to each other. Then you'll draw your version of Wave breaths. Go!

5. Closing

"Let's take a moment to think about something kind you could do for your Kindness pal today. You can close your eyes if you want to."

Wait. *Who has an idea of what you might do?* **Invite a few answers.**

Thanks for a great class, everyone!

Ring a bell or chime if you have one.

Extension: *Peace of Mind Core Curriculum for Grade 3: Lesson 18, Page 108. The Blooming Breaths practice was created by one of Ms. Ryden's students!*

Let's Draw Wave Breathing

What does Wave Breathing look like to you?

|

Lesson 9
Make up Your Own Breath

Slides: 86-96

1. Introduction

You might say: *Today we are going to make up our own way of doing mindful breathing and review the one we learned last time. You'll get to teach your idea to your Kindness Pal.*

2. Mindful Moment

You might ask: *What has been your favorite mindfulness practice so far?* You could ask them to give you a thumbs up for the ones they like as you read off the list: Four Square, Take Five, Gravity Hands, Squeeze and Release, Flower, Visualization, Gratefuls, Wave or one you made up.

Choose the Mindfulness Helper.
You might say: *Today the Mindfulness Helper gets to choose which breath we're going to do.* **Remind** them to say, *"Let's get into our mindful bodies. Let's close our eyes or look down (it's important not to require students to close their eyes). Let's ….."*
Do the practice.
Ring a bell or chime if you have one.

3. American Sign Language (ASL)

You might say: *Today we're going to learn how to say "thirsty" in ASL.* How do you feel in your body when you are thirsty?

Let's watch a video of some Peace of Mind students showing us how to sign "thirsty" **(the video is in the slides)**

ASL Practice
Have everyone try to say "thirsty" in ASL.

4. Kindness Pals

Assign New Kindness Pals. You might say: *Okay it's time to get our new Kindness Pals! There's one important rule of Kindness Pals. Does anybody remember what it is? When I tell you who your Kindness Pal is I want you to say "Okay!" in a nice friendly way.*

Kindness Pal Activity

Remember last time you thought about your own way of doing Wave Breaths? Today you're going to make up your own way of doing Mindful Breathing. It can be anything like Jellyfish Breath, Fireworks Breaths, Baseball Breaths…anything that lets you do simple, slow movements with three deep breaths. Then you'll teach it to your new Kindness Pal and then you're going to draw it. You're going to make a picture just like the ones we've been coloring in Peace Class.

Invite students to draw their own mindful breathing practice on the attached worksheet.

5. Closing

Let's take a moment to think about something kind you could do for your Kindness pal today. You can close your eyes if you want to.

Wait.

Ask: *Who has an idea already of what you might do?* **Invite a few answers.**

Say: *Thanks for a great class, everyone!*

Ring a bell or chime if you have one.

Extension: *Peace of Mind Core Curriculum for Grade 3: Lesson 17, page 102 - Try out Mindful Eating for another way of noticing sensations in your body.*

|

Create Your Own
Mindful Breathing Practice!

My Mindful Breathing Practice is called:

_____

Lesson 10
Sergio Sees the Good

Slides: 97-112

NOTE: For this lesson you will need some small paper cups and marbles, beans, beads, or something small; enough for every Kindness Pal Pair to have 3 cups and about 10 small objects.

1. Introduction

You might say: *Today's lesson will be a little different. I'm going to ask the Mindfulness Helper to choose one of the mindfulness practices we've learned and then we're going to listen to a story. We're going to learn about something called the Negativity Bias, learn how to say "I feel in ASL", and then we're going to do a fun activity with our Kindness Pals.*

2. Mindful Moment

Choose Mindfulness Helper.

Let the mindfulness helper choose and help you to lead a mindfulness practice from all the practices you have learned so far.

Remind them to say, "*Let's get into our mindful bodies. Let's close our eyes or look down* (it's important not to require kids to close their eyes). *Let's* (fill in with chosen practice)....."

Ring a bell or chime if you have one.

3. American Sign Language (ASL)

You might say: *Today we're going to learn how to say "I feel" in ASL. Then we can start to say "I feel happy or I feel sad, etc." Let's watch a video of one of the Peace of Mind students showing us how to sign "I feel."* **(the video is in the slides)**

ASL Practice; Have everyone try to say "I feel" in ASL. Then try adding some of the feeling words you've learned so far.

4. The Brain's Negativity Bias

Read the book or watch the video of Sergio Sees the Good **(8 mins)** OR if you don't have time you can watch this 4 minute video Marleigh Sees the Good.

Discuss

- Do you remember what each marble represents?

- Since the marbles are probably all the same size you might ask whether all of the things that Sergio remembered had the same "weight" or "size". Is waking up in a nice warm bed the same as hearing a funny joke?

- Do we sometimes forget about those big things and take them for granted?

- Have you ever had a day that felt totally ruined? Looking back, do you think that was really true?

- What is the Negativity Bias?

- Do you think our Negativity Bias helps us in any way? (Cactus example)

- Does our Negativity Bias hurt us in any way?

5. Kindness Pals

Assign New Kindness Pals. You might say: *Okay it's time to get our new Kindness Pals! There's one important rule of Kindness Pals. Does anybody remember what it is? When I tell you who your Kindness Pal is I want you to say "Okay!" in a nice friendly way.*

Kindness Pal Activity

Play the Marble Game.

Directions:

- Give each pair of Kindness Pals 3 paper cups and about ten marbles or other small objects. One cup is the "good" cup, one is the "bad" cup, and the other cup holds the small objects.

- Have them take turns.

- One student starts to recount their day to the other student. "I got up but I didn't want to. I put on my favorite shirt. I smelled waffles…"

- The student who's talking identifies each part of their day as good or bad. The student who is listening puts the marbles in the good or bad cups accordingly.

- Have students notice how many marbles are in each cup when all 10 have been used: what kind of day has it really been so far for that student?

- Then they pour the marbles out and switch.

6. **Optional: Work on Sergio's Scales Coloring Sheet with their Kindness Pals**

7. **Closing**

Let's take a moment to think about something kind you could do for your Kindness pal today. You can close your eyes if you want to.
Wait.
Ask*: Who has an idea already of what you might do?* ***Invite a few answers.***
Say*: Thanks for a great class, everyone!*
Ring a bell or chime if you have one.

Extension: *See the back pages in the book <u>Sergio Sees the Good</u> for more about the Negativity Bias and additional gratitude related activities.*

Sergio's Scale

good bad

Share with your Kindness Pal all the little things that happened today and draw a marble on the good side or the bad side for each thing you remember.

Lesson 11
Tell Me Something Good

<u>Slides: 113-122</u>

> **NOTE**: *Before you teach this lesson you can listen to a little bit of this great old song by Chaka Khan. You'll just be singing the chorus. <u>Tell Me Something Good</u> You can start listening at 1:03.* **Do not play the whole song for the class - it's not 3rd grade appropriate!**

1. Introduction

You might say: *Today I'm going to ask the Mindfulness Helper to choose one of the mindfulness practices we've learned. We will learn how to express a new feeling in ASL, and then we're going to play a game all together. Then you're going to make a list of little good things with your Kindness Pals.*

2. Mindful Moment

Choose Mindfulness Helper.
Let the mindfulness helper choose and help you to lead a mindfulness practice from all the practices you have learned so far.
Remind them to say, *"Let's get into our mindful bodies. Let's close our eyes or look down (it's important not to require kids to close their eyes). Let's ….."*
Ring a bell or chime if you have one.

3. American Sign Language (ASL)

You might say: *Today we're going to learn how to say "frustrated" in ASL. How do you feel in your body when you feel frustrated?*

Choose a few volunteers to demonstrate what "frustrated" looks like.

Let's watch a video of one of the Peace of Mind students showing us how to sign "frustrated." **(the video is in the slides)**

ASL Practice: Have everyone try to say "frustrated" in ASL.

4. Gratitude Practice

Play the game Tell Me Something Good!

You might say: *Do you remember the Negativity Bias and how sometimes it can be easy to forget to notice the little good things in our lives? Today we're going to learn a way to hack our Negativity Bias by helping to train our brains to be grateful. And to make it even more fun, we are going to sing a little song about it.*

I'm going to ask you to think of a little good thing in your life. You'll raise your hand when you're ready. When I call on you, we'll all sing Tell Me Something Good! And then you will. Let's try it. I'll go first. Sing it with me: Tell Me Something Good! And I'll tell you that I had waffles for breakfast (insert your own little good thing here). Your turn!

5. Kindness Pals

Assign New Kindness Pals. You might say: *It's time to get our new Kindness Pals! There's one important rule of Kindness Pals. Does anybody remember what it is? When I tell you who your Kindness Pal is I want you to say "Okay!" in a nice friendly way.*

Kindness Pal Activity: *Now we're going to do an activity with your Kindness Pal. When I say "Go!" you're going to find your Kindness Pal and you're going to make a list of Ten Little Good Things. These can be really small things like "when the syrup fills up every little square in the waffle", or "hearing a kitten purr," or "the sound of a bat hitting a baseball," or "opening a new box of cereal." After you and your Kindness Pal have come up with your list we'll share out.*

Closing: *Let's take a moment to think about something kind you could do for your Kindness pal today. You can close your eyes if you want to.* **Wait.** *Who has an idea of what you might do?* **Take a few answers.** *Thanks for a great class, everyone!* **Ring** *bell.*

_____

Extension: *Peace of Mind Core Curriculum for Grade 3: Lesson 8, Page 59, Additional Gratitude Activities.*

Ten Little Good Things

Your Name: _____

1. _____

2. _____

3. _____

4. _____

5. _____

6. _____

7. _____

8. _____

9. _____

10. _____

Lesson 12
Rosie's Brain

Slides: 123-133

1. Introduction

You might say: *Today I'm going to ask the Mindfulness Helper to choose one of the mindfulness practices we've learned, we'll learn a new ASL sign, and then we're going to listen to a story about our brains. Then you're going to spend a little time with your Kindness Pals finding out how much you have in common.*

2. Mindful Moment

Choose the Mindfulness Helper.

Let the mindfulness helper choose and help you to lead a mindfulness practice from all the practices you have learned so far.

Remind them to say, "*Let's get into our mindful bodies. Let's close our eyes or look down (it's important not to require students to close their eyes). Let's (fill in with chosen practice) …..*" **Ring** a bell or chime if you have one.

3. American Sign Language (ASL)

You might say: *Today we're going to learn how to say "excited" in ASL. How do you feel in your body when you feel excited?*

Choose a few volunteers to demonstrate what "excited" looks like.

Let's watch a video of one of the Peace of Mind students showing us how to sign "excited." **(the video is in the slides)**

ASL Practice: Have everyone try to say "excited" in ASL. Does the sign for "excited" match the way your body feels when you are excited?

4. Three Important Parts of the Brain

Read the book or watch the video of <u>Watch Rosie's Brain</u> OR if you don't have time you can watch this 4 min video called <u>Marleigh's Brain.</u>

Discuss: Questions for Rosie's Brain

Why was Rosie angry?

- What did her Amygdala (Amy) want her to do?

- Was Amy's idea (smashing the piano) a good one?

- How did her Hippocampus (Miss Pickles) help her?

- How did her PFC help her?

- Can you think of another way to solve Rosie's problem?

- What parts of your brain do you think you used to answer these questions?

5. Kindness Pals

Assign new Kindness Pals as before.

Kindness Pal Activity: *When I say "Go!" you're going to find your Kindness Pal and then I'm going to give you 30 seconds to find out how many things you have in common. Ask each other about foods you like, animals, colors, books, movies, toys, whatever!*

Who thinks they have the most things in common? Have everyone share one thing that they had in common with their Kindness Pal.

6. Optional: Brain Coloring Sheet

7. Closing

Let's take a moment to think about something kind you could do for your Kindness pal today. You can close your eyes if you want to. **Wait.** *Who has an idea already of what you might do?* ***Invite a few answers.***
Say: *Thanks for a great class, everyone!* **Ring** a bell or chime.

———————————

Extension: *The Peace of Mind Core Curriculum for Grade 3: Unit 6 Brain on Science includes 4 interactive lessons to help students learn more about their amygdala, hippocampus and prefrontal cortex and how to put this knowledge to work in their lives. Page 122.*

49 | | https://TeachPeaceofMind.org

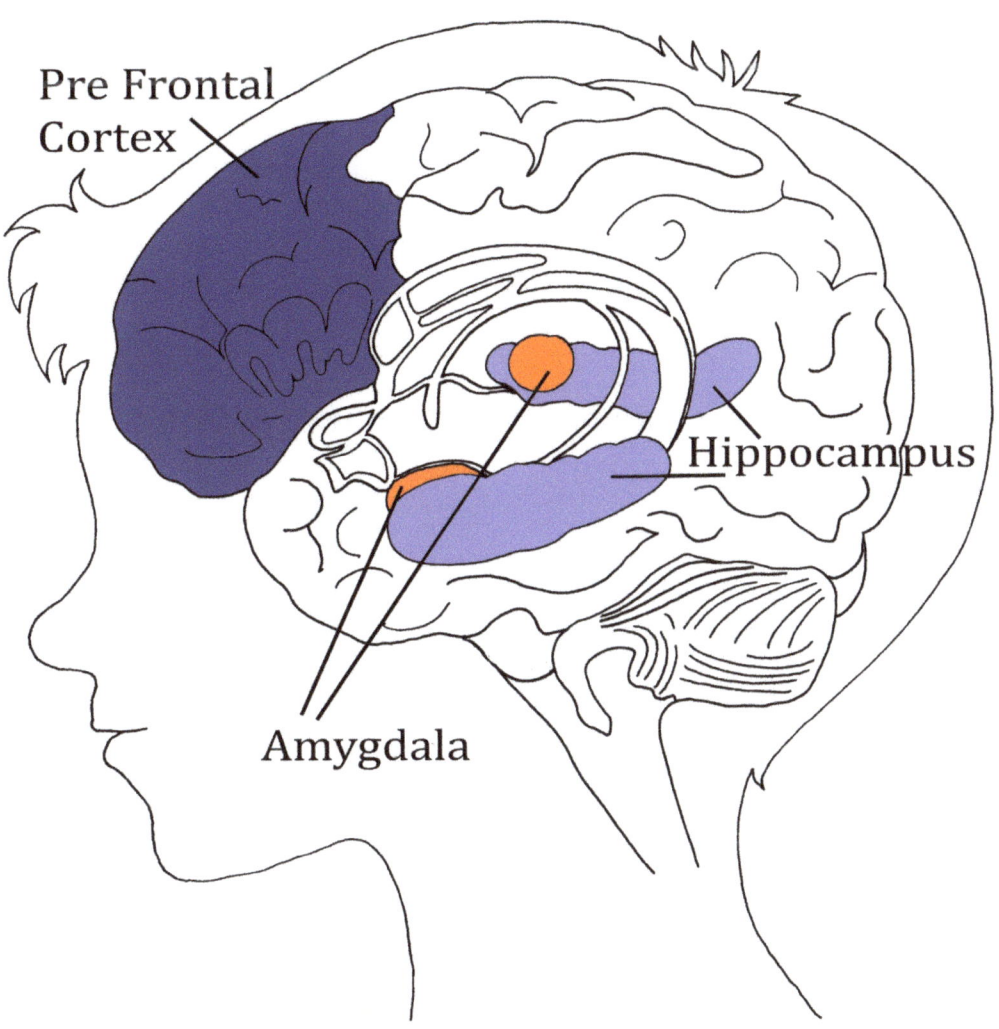

Pre Frontal Cortex

Hippocampus

Amygdala

Lesson 13
Mason and the Conflict CAT

**Slides: 134-144**

1. Introduction

You might say: _Today we're going to do our mindfulness practice and learn a new ASL sign after we read a story. The mindfulness practice for today will be taught in the story. Today we're going to read a book about conflict. It's called Mason and the Conflict CAT. What do you think the word "conflict" means? What do you think the Conflict CAT is? Does the cover of the book give you any clues?_

2. Conflict Resolution

Read the book or <u>watch the video of Mason and the Conflict CAT</u>.

Discuss

- What is a conflict?
- What was the conflict in the story?
- What made the conflict get better?
- Did some of the kids say things that made the conflict worse?
- Did all of the kids make the conflict bigger?
- What is the Conflict CAT? What do the letters stand for?
- How did the kids calm down?
- Why is it important to apologize?
- What were some of the tools in the Toolbox?
- What tool did the kids use to work out their conflict?
- Did everybody get exactly what they wanted?
- Is it okay if you don't get exactly what you want if you still get something pretty good?
- Do you ever have conflicts?
- How do you usually handle them?
- Could you imagine using the Conflict CAT?

3. Mindful Moment

Let's try Candle Breathing Now!

Choose Mindfulness Helper.

Remind them to say, *"Let's get into our mindful bodies. Let's close our eyes or look down (it's important not to require students to close their eyes). Let's try Candle Breathing now. Help them lead the practice.*

Ring a bell or chime if you have one.

4. American Sign Language (ASL)

You might say: *Today we're going to learn how to say "How are you feeling today?" in ASL. Then we'll be able to ask each other about how we are feeling and answer!*

Let's watch a video of some Peace of Mind students showing us how to sign "How are you feeling today?." **(the video is in the slides)**

ASL Practice: Have everyone try to say "How are you feeling today?" in ASL.

5. Kindness Pals

Assign new Kindness Pals as before.

Kindness Pal Activity: *When I say "Go!" you're going to find your Kindness Pal and share a time that you have been in a conflict. How did you solve it?*

Invite a few pairs to share out.

6. Closing

Let's take a moment to think about something kind you could do for your Kindness pal today. You can close your eyes if you want to. **Wait.** *Who has an idea already of what you might do?* ***Invite a few answers.***

Say: *Thanks for a great class, everyone!* **Ring** *a bell or chime.*

Extension: *Peace of Mind Core Curriculum for Grade 3: Unit 7 includes 8 full lessons on Conflict Resolution. P. 144*

The Conflict C.A.T.

Candle Breathing

Imagine you are blowing out the
candles on your birthday cake.
Take three slow deep breaths.

Lesson 14
Practice Using the Conflict CAT

Slides: 145-155

1. Introduction

You might say: *Today I'm going to ask the Mindfulness Helper to choose our mindfulness practice and then we're going to practice using the Conflict CAT. We're going to act out a story and then you're going to play a game with your Kindness Pals called Nine Words.*

2. Mindful Moment

Choose the Mindfulness Helper.

Let the mindfulness helper choose and help you to lead a mindfulness practice from all the practices you have learned so far.

Remind them to say, *"Let's get into our mindful bodies. Let's close our eyes or look down (it's important not to require kids to close their eyes). Let's ….."*

Ring a bell or chime if you have one.

3. American Sign Language (ASL)

You might say: Today we're going to learn how to say "hungry" in ASL. How do you feel in your body when you are hungry?

Let's watch a video of some Peace of Mind students showing us how to sign "hungry." **(the video is in the slides)**

ASL Practice

Have everyone try to say "hungry" in ASL.

4. Conflict Resolution

Review the Conflict CAT

Ask:

- Who remembers what the letters CAT stand for in the Conflict CAT?

- What was the conflict that Mason and his friends had?

- Who can remember some of the tools in the Conflict Toolbox?

- What tool did Mason and his friends use to work out their conflict?

Practice using the Conflict CAT

You might say: *Today we are going to act out a conflict. I'm going to choose two of you to act out the story about siblings named Zion and Zuri. We're going to do two versions of the same story.*

Act it Out: Fun Saturday (1)

Choose two students to act out the story and ask them to pantomime what you are describing in the story — if you say they are jumping up and down, the students will jump up and down.

You will be the narrator. You will read their lines and then the students can repeat the lines after you read them.

The script to read aloud is on the following page.

Fun Saturday
(Version 1) with siblings Zuri and Zion

Narrator: *Every Saturday morning **Zuri** and **Zion** go to the park. **Zuri** and **Zion** LOVE Saturday mornings!*

They love to play basketball. (act out playing basketball).

They love to go on the swings. (act out playing on the swings, etc.)

They love to climb trees. They love to ride bikes.

They love to count ladybugs. They love to play in the water fountain.

They love to do the monkey bars.

> *Have the kids suggest more things for Zion and Zuri to do at the park and have the kids act them out.*

Narrator: *Last week **Zuri** was able to get all the way across the monkey bars for the first time and she really wanted to do it again this week.*

*But **Zion** had been dreaming about splashing in the fountain all during this hot week.*

***Zuri** said, "Let's go to the monkey bars! I can't wait to try going all the way across!"*

***Zion** said, "No! I'm hot! I want to splash in the fountain!"*

***Zuri** said, "But Mom said we have to stay together! And I want to go to the monkey bars!" **Zuri** was starting to get frustrated now. Her face was getting hot and her body felt tight and tense.*

***Zion** was angry. He always had to watch his younger sister. Sometimes it made him feel frustrated. He could feel that frustrated feeling in his belly. He said, "The monkey bars are boring! I've been going across since I was 6 years old!"*

***Zuri** was really mad now. She said, "You're a show-off! Big brothers are the worst!"*

***Zion** was angry too. He said, "No, you're the worst!"*

***Zuri** said, "What?! I'm going to tell Mom that you're the meanest brother ever!"*

***Zion** said, "Fine with me!"*

They both stormed off and sat on separate benches for the rest of the morning.

The End.

Discuss

- What is the conflict between Zion and Zuri?

- How can you tell that they are getting angry? (Body language, yelling.)

- What part of Zuri and Zion's brains are controlling their actions? (Remind them of Rosie's Brain) (Amygdala.)

- Has their amygdala chosen fight, flight, or freeze?

- How is that choice working out for them?

- What part of their brains would help them work this conflict out peacefully? (The prefrontal cortex.)

- If they were using their PFCs, how could they solve this conflict?

Take a few answers.

Act it Out: Fun Saturday (Version 2)
You might say: *Now we are going to act out the story of Zion and Zuri again but we are going to write new endings to the story.*

Choose two new volunteers to be Zuri and Zion.

Invite the volunteers to act out the story (above) as you read.

Freeze the action at various points to ask the class for suggestions about how to solve their conflicts.

If they don't suggest them, offer these ideas:
- They could take turns playing on the monkey bars and then the fountain.

- One of them could offer to do what the other one wants to do out of simple kindness.

- They could compromise and do something else, like play on the swings.

    Ask: Would things have turned out better for the Zuri and Zion if they had tried some of our ideas?

5. Kindness Pals

Assign New Kindness Pals as before.

Kindness Pal Activity *When I say "Go!" you're going to find your Kindness Pal and play Nine Words. You're going to try to come up with nine words that start with the first letter of each one of your names. You need to think of three foods, three animals, and three of anything at all.*

For example, if my name is Linda and your name is Jeremiah, then we have to think of three foods that start with L and three foods that start with J, three animals that start with L and three animals that start with J, and then three of anything that start with L and with J. L: Linguine, Lollipops, Lettuce, J: Jam, Jelly, Jellybeans.

6. Closing

Let's take a moment to think about something kind you could do for your Kindness pal today. You can close your eyes if you want to. **Wait.** *Who has an idea already of what you might do?* ***Invite a few answers.***

Say: *Thanks for a great class, everyone!* **Ring** a bell or chime.

Extension: *Peace of Mind Core Curriculum for Grade 3: Lesson 13, Page 82, for another skit to practice solving conflicts peacefully.*

Lesson 15
Kindness Taps

Slides: 156-166

1. Introduction

You might say: _Today is our last Peace of Mind session together. I've really enjoyed learning about mindfulness, brain science and conflict resolution with you. I hope you have enjoyed Peace Class too! Today we're going to learn a different kind of mindfulness practice called Heartfulness._

Heartfulness is kind of like an experiment - you see what it feels like to think kind things about people. You notice how it makes you feel. Scientists have shown that people who do this practice regularly are usually kinder to others and to themselves. Let's see what happens when we try it. Then we'll play a game all together.

2. Mindful Moment

Choose Mindfulness Helper. Help them lead Heartfulness practice.

Watch the Jonah Heartfulness Video.

Remind the Mindfulness Helper one last time to say, "_Let's get into our mindful bodies. Let's close our eyes or look down_ (it's important not to require kids to close their eyes). _Let's send kind thoughts to someone you care about who you've seen yesterday or today; to ourselves; to our whole class. May (you/I/ we all) be happy; May (you/I/we) be healthy and strong; May (you/I/we/all) be peaceful. Take one more deep breath in and out._
Ring a bell or chime if you have one.

Share: Ask if anyone wants to share what that felt like. Ask if anybody wants to share who they were sending their kind thoughts to.

3. American Sign Language (ASL)

You might say: _Today we're going to learn how to say "loved" in ASL. How do you feel in your body when you feel loved?_

Choose a few volunteers to demonstrate what "loved" looks like.

Let's watch a video of one of the Peace of Mind students showing us how to sign "loved". **(the video is in the slides)**

ASL Practice: Have everyone try to say "loved" in ASL. Point out that the sign involves our faces, hand gestures and body motions. Ask them if the sign matches the way that they feel when they feel loved.

4. Kindness Pals

Assign New Kindness Pals

You might say: *It's time to get our new Kindness Pals - for the last time! There's one important rule of Kindness Pals. Does anybody remember what it is? When I tell you who your Kindness Pal is I want you to say "Okay!" in a nice friendly way.*

Kindness Pal Activity
Kindness Taps

This activity is designed to help children share the kindness they have been practicing in the previous 14 lessons in a new way.

Instructions:

Split your class in half. One half sits with their heads down and eyes closed (the sitters should sit evenly spread across the room so students aren't crowded together and others can walk around them). The other half stands in the back of the room (the standers).

The standers will walk around the room and gently tap students on the shoulder who they feel fit the identity of the person in the statements being read by the teacher. The teacher will read each of the following statements one at a time, giving 15-30 seconds after each statement to let the standers walk around and tap all the students they wish. Standers can tap any and all of the sitters. There's no limit that you can only tap one student per statement. During the walking/tapping time, the teacher is encouraged to monitor and tap students who they feel aren't getting as many taps as other students. The expectation is that students are doing this activity quietly.

Statements (feel free to add your own):

"This person makes me smile when I see them in the morning."

"This person has taught me something."

"This person has made me laugh or smile."

"This person has helped me feel better on a day I wasn't feeling my best."

"This person has pleasantly surprised me."

"I enjoy spending time with this person."

"I want to get to know this person better."

"I am grateful this person is in my class."

Switch sitters and standers. Repeat the exercise!

5. **Share: What surprised you about what you got tapped for? What made you feel happy?**

6. **Closing**

    This is our last class together. I hope that you enjoyed learning more about mindfulness, kindness, and how to work out our conflicts peacefully. The world needs lots of kind, mindful people. Now you have some tools to help you go out into the world and make it a more peaceful place. I hope you will!

    Thank you so much for a wonderful time together!

Heartfulness

Who did you think your kind thoughts about?
Draw or write about them below.

May you be happy.
May you be healthy and strong.
May you be peaceful.

About Linda Ryden, Author

Linda Ryden is the author of seven mindfulness-based children's books published by Cherry Lake Publishing and Peace of Mind Inc. Linda is the founder and Creative Director of Peace of Mind Inc. and creator of the Peace of Mind Program and author of the Peace of Mind Curriculum Series, a cutting-edge combination of mindfulness-based social-emotional learning, conflict resolution and social justice for Early Childhood through Middle School.Linda served as the full-time Peace Teacher at Lafayette Elementary School, Washington DC's largest public elementary school from 2003 to 2023, teaching Peace of Mind classes to more than 700 students every week.

Linda's work has been featured in The Washington Post, Washingtonian Magazine, Washington Parent, Washington Family, Teaching Tolerance, and Edutopia, among others. Linda was a keynote speaker at the National Network of State Teachers of the Year conference and a featured speaker at the National Education Association Foundation Symposium, and has received a Commendation for Educational Innovation from the DC Board of Education.

Linda lives in Washington D.C. with her husband Jeremiah Cohen, owner of Bullfrog Bagels, and their dog Phoebe.

In that small but growing band of peace educators, Linda Ryden stands out. The glistening ideas and stories in these pages are sure to open minds and stir hearts, in much the way that has been happening all these years with the children in her classrooms.

— Colman McCarthy, Founder of The Center for Teaching Peace

Bibliography

Bradshaw, C. P. (2015). Translating research to practice in bullying prevention. American Psychologist, 70 (4), 322-332.

Breeding, K., & Harrison, J. (2007). Connected and Respected: Lessons from the Resolving Conflict Creatively Program. Cambridge, Mass.: Educators for Social Responsibility.

Durlak, J. A., Weissberg, R. P., Dymnicki, A. B., Taylor, R. D. & Schellinger, K. B. (2011). The impact of enhancing students' social and emotional learning: A meta-analysis of school-based universal interventions. Child Development, 82(1): 405–432.

Hanson, R. (2015). Hardwiring Happiness. Random House USA.

Jennings, P. (2015). Mindfulness for teachers: Simple skills for peace and productivity in the classroom. The Norton Series on the Social Neuroscience of Education.

Jennings, P. A. (2019). The Trauma-Sensitive Classroom: Building Resilience with Compassionate Teaching. New York: W.W. Norton & Company.

Lantieri, Linda. "How SEL and Mindfulness Can Work Together." Greater Good. April 7, 2015. Accessed September 28, 2015. http://greatergood.berkeley.edu/article/item/how_social_emotional_learning_and_mindfulness_can_work_together.

Learning Heroes, Developing Life Skills in Children: A Road Map for Communicating with Parents, https://bealearninghero.org/parent-mindsets/ September 2018

O'Brennan, L., & Bradshaw, C. (2013). School Climate: A Research Brief. A report prepared for the National Education Association, Washington, DC.

Rechtschaffen, D., & Kabat-Zinn PhD, J. (2014). The Way of Mindful Education: Cultivating Well-being in Teachers and Students. Norton Books in Education. Schonert-Reichl, K. A., & Lawlor, M. S. (2010). The effects of a mindfulness-based education program on pre-and early adolescents' well-being and social and emotional competence. Mindfulness, 1(3), 137-151.

Schonert-Reichl, K. A., Oberle, E., Lawlor, M. S., Abbott, D., Thomson, K., Oberlander, T. F., & Diamond, A. (2015). Enhancing cognitive and social–emotional development through a simple-to-administer mindfulness-based school program for elementary school children: A randomized controlled trial. Developmental Psychology, 51(1), 52-66.

Seppala, E., Simon-Thomas, E., Brown, S. L., Worline, M. C., Cameron, C. D., & Doty, J. R. (2017). The Oxford Handbook of Compassion Science. New York, NY: Oxford University Press.

Siegel, D. J., & Bryson, T. P. (2012). The Whole-Brain Child. London: Constable & Robinson.

Simmons, Dena (2019), Why We Can't Afford Whitewashed Social-Emotional Learning Retrieved from http://www.ascd.org/publications/newsletters/education_update/apr19/vol61/num04

Srinivasan, M. (2014). Teach, Breathe, Learn: Mindfulness in and out of the Classroom. Berkeley, CA: Parallax Press.

Treleaven, David (2018). Trauma-Sensitive Mindfulness: Practices for Safe and Transformative Healing. New York: W. W. Norton & Company.

Weare, K. (2013). Developing mindfulness with children and young people: A review of the evidence and policy context. Journal of Children's Services, 8(2), 141-153.

Zoogman, S., Goldberg, S.B., Hoyt, W.T., & Miller, L. (2015). Mindfulness interventions with youth: A meta-analysis. Mindfulness, 6, 290 - 302.

Zenner, C., Hermleben-Kurz, S., & Walach, H. (2014). Mindfulness-based interventions in schools: A systematic review and meta-analysis. Frontiers in Psychology, 5, article 603.

Appreciation

Peace of Mind is based in our community, and we are so lucky to have the support and guidance and help of so many wonderful people. We are grateful to Mike Di Marco, Valentina Gabrielli and the teachers and staff of Horizons Greater Washington for inspiring us to create this curriculum and being our first pilot program in summer 2024. A fantastic group of educators in the DC area and beyond piloted the Flex Curriculum during the 24-25 school year and provided helpful feedback. This curriculum wouldn't exist without many wonderful friends of Peace of Mind including Kelly Gilstrap, Jillian Diesner, Jodi Ferrier, Elie Goldman, Jennifer Greene, our friends at Metamer Studios, and the students who helped to create the amazing ASL and mindfulness videos. As always, we are able to do what we do at Peace of Mind thanks to the support of very generous foundations and kind individual donors! Thank you!!